Table of Contents

Food and Drink

- I'm on a seafood diet.

I see food, and I eat it!

- What do you call a fake noodle?

An impasta!

- Why don't eggs tell jokes?

They'd crack each other up!

- Why did the cheese go to the gym?

To get shredded!

- What do you call a sad cheese?

Blue cheese!

- How do you get a Swiss cheese to stop?

You brie-be it!

- What did the baby cheese say when its picture was taken?

Cheese!

- Why was the cheese looking so down?

It was feeling blue!

- What do you call dangerous precipitation?

Hail storm cheese!

- How do you handle dangerous cheese?

Caerphilly!

😝

- What did the cheese say to itself in the mirror?

Halloumi!

😝

- Why did the yogurt go to the art exhibit?

Because it was cultured!

- What cheese is made backwards?

Edam!

😝

- Why did the tomato blush?

Because it saw the salad dressing!

😝

- What do you call a sad strawberry?

A blueberry!

- Why did the baby corn call for its mommy?

It was feeling popped!

- How do you make an apple turnover?

Push it downhill!

- Why did the cucumber blush?

Because it saw the salad undressing!

- What do you call a vegetable that's rough around the edges?

Broccoli!

- Why did the mushroom go to the party?

Because he was a fun guy!

- How do you fix a broken tomato?

With tomato paste!

- What do you call a fancy lemon?

Sophis-ticated!

😝

- Why did the grape stop in the middle of the road?

Because it ran out of juice!

😝

- What did the ice cream say to the unhappy cake?

"What's eating you?"

- Why was the cookie crying?

Because its mother had been a wafer so long!

- What do you call a dessert that's always nervous?

Panna cotta!

- Why did the pie go to the dentist?

Because it needed a filling!

- What do you call a fake noodle dessert?

An im-pastry!

😝

- Why did the cupcake go to the doctor?

It was feeling a little batter!

😝

- What did one scoop say to the other scoop?

"Want to spoon?"

- Why was the cake so embarrassed?

It was in tiers!

- What do you call a dessert that's always complaining?

A whiney tart!

- Why did the donut go to the therapist?

It felt hole inside!

- Why did the cookie go to the nurse?

Because it was feeling crumbly!

- What do you call a fake pasta dish?

Spa-phony!

- Why did the banana go to the doctor?

It wasn't peeling well!

Animals

- What do you call a cold dog?

A Chilli dog!

😝

- Why don't cats play poker in the jungle?

Too many cheetahs!

😝

- What do you call a cat that lives in an igloo?

An eskimew!

- Why did the dog get a job at the bank?

He wanted to be a watchdog!

- What do you call a cat wearing shoes?

Puss in boots!

- Why don't dogs make good dancers?

Because they have two left feet!

- What do you call a flying cat?

A purr-plane!

- Why did the cat join the Red Cross?

Because she wanted to be a first-aid kit!

- Why don't cats ever make spelling mistakes?

They always check their litter-ature!

- Why did the cow cross the road?

To get to the udder side!

- What do you call a sleeping bull?

A bulldozer!

- Why did the farmer name his pig "Ink"?

Because it kept running out of the pen!

- What do you call a chicken staring at a lettuce?

Chicken sees a salad!

- Why did the sheep say "meow"?

It was learning a new language!

- Why did the rooster go to the bakery?

He needed a new comb!

- What do you call a pig that does karate?

A pork chop!

- Why did the horse go behind the tree?

To change his jockeys!

- What do you call a cow with a sense of humor?

Laughing stock!

- Why don't oysters donate to charity?

Because they're shellfish!

😝

- What do you call a bear with no ears?

B!

😝

- How do you catch a squirrel?

Climb a tree and act like a nut!

- Why don't ants get sick?

Because they have tiny ant-ibodies!

- What do you call a sleeping dinosaur?

A dino-snore!

- Why don't crabs give to charity?

Because they're shellfish!

- What do you call a monkey that loves potato chips?

A chipmunk!

- How do you make an octopus laugh?

With ten-tickles!

- What do you call a lazy kangaroo?

A pouch potato!

- Why don't sharks eat clowns?

Because they taste funny!

😝

- What do you call a fish wearing gym shoes?

Sole-mon!

😝

- How does a penguin build its baseball field?

Igloos it together!

Wordplay and Puns

- Why did the letter "C" need glasses?

Because it couldn't C very well!

- What starts with "e," ends with "e," and contains one letter?

An envelope!

- How do you make the number one disappear?

Add the letter "g" and it's "gone"!

- What do you call a word spelled incorrectly in the dictionary?

Wrong!

- What do you call a pile of cats?

A meowtain!

- What do you call a bee that can't make up its mind?

A maybe!

- What do you call a dinosaur with an extensive vocabulary?

A thesaurus!

- What do you call two banana peels?

A pair of slippers!

- What do you call a sibling who refuses to share their French fries?

Selfish potato!

- What do you call a brother who sings?

A bro-calist!

😝

- What do you call a sibling who's always borrowing money?

A loan ranger!

😝

- What do you call a grandpa who's always ready to go?

Gramps to go!

- What do you call a grandparent who can bench press 300 pounds?

Gran-ite!

- What do you call a grandma who tells jokes?

Nanna-rator!

- What's a grandparent's favorite type of phone?

A gran-droid!

- What do you call a grandpa with a rubber toe?

Roberto!

- What do you call a bear doing crunches?

A belly bear!

- What do you call a fish wearing gym shoes?

Sole-mon!

- What do you call a welder on their day off?

A fuse-ionaire!

- What do you call a doctor who fixes websites?

A URL-ologist!

- What do you call a psychic little person who has escaped from prison?

A small medium at large!

- What do you call a priest who becomes a lawyer?

A father-in-law!

- What do you call a veterinarian with laryngitis?

A hoarse doctor!

- What do you call a computer floating in the ocean?

A Dell rolling in the deep!

- What do you call a smartphone that snitches?

A tattle-phone!

😝

- What do you call a phone that tells jokes?

Cell-arious!

😝

- What do you call a group of musical smartphones?

A cell-phone-y!

- What do you call a computer mouse that swears?

Cursors!

😝

- What do you call a scared Santa?

Claus-trophobic!

😝

- What do you call an elf wearing earmuffs?

Anything you want, he can't hear you!

- What do you call a kid who doesn't believe in Santa?

A rebel without a Claus!

- What do you call a fat pumpkin?

A plumpkin!

- What do you call a witch at the beach?

A sand-witch!

- What do you call a ghost's true love?

His ghoul-friend!

- What do you call a bunny with fleas?

Bugs Bunny!

- What do you call a Dad on Valentine's Day?

Apparent heart!

- What do you call a boomerang that doesn't come back?

A stick!

- What do you call a belt made of watches?

A waist of time!

- What do you call a fake watch?

A counterfeit timepiece!

- What do you call a dinosaur that never gives up?

Try-ceratops!

- What do you call a sleeping computer?

A laptop!

- What do you call a sad fruit?

A blueberry!

- What do you call a bear in the rain?

A drizzly bear!

😝

- What do you call a lion who's obsessed with the past?

Mufasa-bout history!

😝

- What do you call a bee that lives in America?

A USB!

- What do you call a fake Irish stone?

A sham-rock!

😝

Science and Nature

- Why don't scientists trust atoms?

They make up everything!

😝

- How do you organize a space party?

You planet!

😝

- How do you know it's a dogwood tree?

By its bark?

- What do you call a tree that doubts autumn?

Disbe-leaf!

- Why did the gardener plant light bulbs?

They wanted to grow a power plant!

- What do trees wear to pool parties?

Swimming trunks!

- How do trees access the internet?

They log in!

😝

- What did the little tree say to the big tree?

Leaf me alone!

😝

- Why don't mountains get cold in the winter?

They wear snow caps!

- Why did the tree go to the dentist?

It needed a root canal!

- Why don't scientists trust stairs?

They're always up to something!

Sports

- What do you call a soccer player with a vocabulary?

A goal with words!

- Why did the basketball player bring a ladder to the game?

He wanted to get a higher score!

- How do baseball players stay cool?

They sit next to their fans!

- Why was the baseball player such a good singer?

He could hit all the pitches!

😝

- What's a tennis player's favorite type of music?

A serve-vey!

😝

- Why was the football coach against his daughter dating?

He didn't want her to receiver!

- What do you call a pig that plays basketball?

A ball hog!

- Why don't tennis players ever get married?

Because love means nothing to them!

- What's a hiker's favorite type of music?

Trail mix!

Technology & Computers

- Why was the computer cold?

It left its Windows open!

- What's a computer's favorite snack?

Microchips!

- How does a computer get drunk?

It takes screenshots!

- Why was the computer late to work?

It had a hard drive!

- What did the computer do at lunchtime?

Had a byte!

- What do you call a computer floating in the ocean?

A Dell rolling in the deep!

- How do you comfort a JavaScript bug?

You console it!

- What's a computer's favorite beat?

An algo-rhythm!

- Why did the smartphone go to the dentist?

Because it had Bluetooth!

- What do you call a smartphone that snitches?

A tattle-phone!

- Why did the cell phone quit its job?

It just wasn't ringing true anymore.

- What do you call a phone that tells jokes?

Cell-arious!

- Why was the smartphone stressed out?

Too many pocket dials!

- What do you call a smartphone with no service?

An expensive paperweight!

- Why did the iPhone go to therapy?

It had too many emotional baggage apps!

- How does a smartphone propose?

With a ring tone!

- What do you call a group of musical smartphones?

A cell-phone-y!

- Why did the Android phone break up with the iPhone?

It couldn't handle the long-distance char-ges!

- Why was the internet addicted to the bakery website?

It loved browsing!

😝

- How does a network admin get drunk?

By taking a few routing shots!

😝

- What do you call a computer mouse that swears?

Cursors!

- Why did the Wi-Fi and the computer get married?

They had a connection!

- What do you call it when you have too many emails?

You've got mail-function!

- What do you call a sad browser?

Internet Explore-er!

- Why don't web developers like nature?

Too many bugs and no debugging tools!

😝

- What did the router say to the doctor?

It's feeling a bit disconnected lately!

😝

Holidays & Seasons

- What do you call a scared Santa?

Claus-trophobic!

- Why does Santa have three gardens?

So he can 'ho ho ho'!

- What do elves learn in school?

The elf-abet!

- Why did Rudolph the red-nosed reindeer win the lottery?

He had the most doe!

😝

- What do you call an elf wearing earmuffs?

Anything you want, he can't hear you!

😝

- Why did the Christmas tree go to the barber?

It needed to be trimmed!

- Why was the snowman looking through the carrots?

He was picking his nose!

- What do you call a kid who doesn't believe in Santa?

A rebel without a Claus!

- How does Christmas Day end?

With the letter 'Y'!

- What do you call a fat pumpkin?

A plumpkin!

😝

- Why didn't the skeleton go to the Halloween party?

He had no body to go with!

😝

- What do you call a witch at the beach?

A sand-witch!

- Why don't mummies take time off?

They're afraid to unwind!

- What do ghosts wear when their eyesight gets blurry?

Spook-tacles!

- How do monsters tell their future?

They read their horrorscope!

- What's a vampire's favorite fruit?

A blood orange!

😝

- Why did the headless horseman go into business?

He wanted to get ahead in life!

😝

- What do you call a ghost's true love?

His ghoul-friend!

- Why did the zombie go to the dentist?

To improve his bite!

- Why did the Easter egg hide?

It was a little chicken!

- What do you call a bunny with fleas?

Bugs Bunny!

- Why shouldn't you tell an Easter egg a joke?

It might crack up!

- What do you call a Dad on Valentine's Day?

Apparent heart!

- Why do leprechauns love to garden?

They have green thumbs!

- Why was the Thanksgiving turkey the drummer in a band?

It had the drumsticks!

- Why did Cupid hang up his bow and arrow?

He didn't have the heart for it anymore!

- What season is it when you're on a trampoline?

Spring-time!

Professions

- Why are construction workers great at parties?

They really raise the roof!

- What did the electrician say to her apprentice?

You have a lot of potential!

- Why did the plumber carry a wrench to math class?

To work out the leaks in his logic!

- How do carpenters communicate?

With car-penter phones!

- What do you call a welder on their day off?

A fuse-ionaire!

- Why was the HVAC technician always cold?

He was surrounded by cool customers!

- What's a mechanic's favorite drink?

Transmission fluid!

- Why did the roofer bring a ladder to the bar?

He heard the drinks were on the house!

- How does a janitor say goodbye?

Sweep dreams!

- What did one wall say to the other wall during construction?

I'll meet you at the corner!

- Why did the lawyer wake up in a hospital?

He was in critical condition!

- Why don't architects like yoga?

They have truss issues!

- Why did the accountant divorce the banker?

They couldn't reconcile their differences!

- What do you call a psychic little person who has escaped from prison?

A small medium at large!

- Why did the archaeologist go bankrupt?

His career was in ruins!

- What do you call a priest who becomes a lawyer?

A father-in-law!

- Why did the botanist start a business?

To make some green!

- What do you call a veterinarian with laryngitis?

A hoarse doctor!

- What kind of music do planets listen to at work?

Neptunes!

😝

- Why don't programmers like nature?

It has too many bugs.

😝

- How do executives take their coffee?

Decaf-einated!

- What did the envelope say to the stamp at the post office?

Stick with me and we'll go places!

- What do you call a factory that makes okay products?

A satisfactory!

- Why did the computer go to the doctor?

It had a virus!

- Why did the scarecrow become a successful weatherman?

He was outstanding in his field!

- Why did the scarecrow win the Nobel prize?

He was out standing in his field!

Family & Relationships

- What do you call a mom who can't draw?

Tracy.

- Why did the parent bring a ladder to school?

They wanted to help their child get to the next grade!

- What did the big flower say to the little flower?

Hey, bud!

- Why don't twins ever win races?

Because they always tie!

- What do you call two banana peels?

A pair of slippers!

- Why was the younger brother jealous of his older sibling?

Because he always got hand-me-downs, but never hand-me-ups!

- What do you call a sibling who refuses to share their French fries?

Selfish potato!

- Why did the sibling bring a ladder to the argument?

To reach a higher level of understanding!

- What do you call a brother who sings?

A bro-calist!

- Why did the sister share her umbrella?

She wanted to be a great rain-bow!

- What do you call a sibling who's always borrowing money?

A loan ranger!

- Why don't siblings ever get lost?

They always have each other's backs!

- Why don't grandma's teeth ever get cold?

Because she has wisdom warmers!

- What do you call a grandpa who's always ready to go?

Gramps to go!

- Why did grandma start using Instagram?

She heard it was great for preserving memories!

- What do you call a grandparent who can bench press 300 pounds?

Gran-ite!

- Why did grandpa put his money in the blender?

He wanted to make liquid assets!

- What do you call a grandma who tells jokes?

Nanna-rator!

- Why did grandpa wear two pairs of pants when he painted the house?

He wanted to avoid any see-through mishaps!

- What's a grandparent's favorite type of phone?

A gran-droid!

- Why did grandma knit a GPS?

She wanted to make sure grandpa never got purled!

- What do you call a grandpa with a rubber toe?

Roberto!

Weather and Nature

- What do you call a wet bear?

A drizzly bear!

😝

- Why did the man put his money in the freezer?

He wanted cold hard cash for a rainy day!

😝

- What do you call a rabbit caught in a downpour?

A drownpour bunny!

- Why did the cloud stay home?

It was feeling under the weather!

- What do you call a storm that's good at chess?

A rain of terror!

- How does a hurricane see?

With its eye!

- What do you call it when it rains chickens and ducks?

Fowl weather!

- Why did the meteorologist break up with her boyfriend?

He mist the point!

- What do you call a dog caught in a rainstorm?

A drooling machine!

- Why did the umbrella go to therapy?

It had too many issues to open up about!

- What do you call a snowman with a six-pack?

An abdominal snowman!

- Why do fish live in saltwater?

Because pepper makes them sneeze!

- What did the sun say to the other sun?

You're the light of my life!

- Why did the sun go to school?

To get brighter!

- What do you call a fake sun?

An imi-tater!

- How do you talk to a hot sun?

Use SPF (Sun Protection Phrases)!

- Why did the sunscreen go to the party?

To avoid getting burned!

- What do you call a sun that tells dad jokes?

A pun-shine!

- Why did the sun break up with the moon?

It needed some space!

- How does the sun listen to music?

On heat waves!

- What did the beach say to the tide?

Long time, no sea!

- Why don't suns ever go on vacation?

They're always burning up their days off!

😝

Fitness and Health

- Why did the weightlifter quit his job?

He didn't have the strength to carry on!

😝

- Why don't eggs exercise?

They'd crack under the pressure!

😝

- What do you call a dinosaur that never gives up on its workout?

Try-ceratops!

- Why did the cookie go to the gym?

To get a little more chip!

- How do bodybuilders make phone calls?

They dial-up!

- What do you call a bear doing crunches?

A belly bear!

- Why did the treadmill go to the bank?

To run some errands!

- What do you call a fish wearing gym shoes?

Sole-mon!

Miscellaneous

- I wondered why the baseball was getting bigger.

Then it hit me.

😝

- Did you hear about the claustrophobic astronaut?

He just needed a little space.

😝

- Why did the gym close down?

It just didn't work out.

- What do you call a parade of rabbits hopping backwards?

A receding hare-line!

😝

- Why did the scarecrow win an award?

He was outstanding in his field.

😝

- Why can't a nose be 12 inches long?

Because then it would be a foot!

- What do you call a dog magician?

A labracadabrador!

- Why did the golfer bring two pairs of pants?

In case he got a hole in one!

- What do you call a dentist who doesn't like tea?

Denis!

- Why was the broom late?

It over swept!

- Why did the man run around his bed?

He was trying to catch up on his sleep!

- Why was the math book sad?

Because it had too many problems.

- How do you communicate with a fish?

You drop it a line!

- How do you make a campfire laugh?

Tell it a fire cracker!

- Why did the picnic basket go to therapy?

It had too many issues to unpack!

- Why did the belt go to prison?

For holding up a pair of pants!

- Why did the picture go to jail?

Because it was framed!

- How do you make a tissue dance?

You put a little boogie in it!

- Why did the coffee file a police report?

Because it got mugged!

- Why did the invisible man turn down the job offer?

He couldn't see himself doing it!

- Why did the calculator break up with the pencil?

It just couldn't count on him!

- Why couldn't the sailor play cards?

Because he was sitting on the deck!

Thank You for purchasing my book.

It means a lot.

I would be very grateful if You could leave an honest review on product page, after You spend some time with it.

Printed in Great Britain
by Amazon

60746895R00060